CRABS

CRABS

by Sylvia A. Johnson

Photographs by Atsushi Sakurai

A Lerner Natural Science Book

Lerner Publications Company ▪ Mi

Sylvia A. Johnson, Series Editor

Translation of original text by Chaim Uri

Additional photographs by: pp. 10, 14, 15, 43,
S. Arthur Reed, Department of Zoology, University of Hawaii;
pp. 29, 32, 39, Yasuyuki Koike.

The publisher wishes to thank James R. Smail, Professor of Biology,
Macalester College, for his assistance in the preparation of this book.

The glossary on page 46 gives definitions and pronunciations
of words shown in **bold type** in the text.

LIBRARY OF CONGRESS CATALOGING IN PUBLICATION DATA

Johnson, Sylvia A.
  Crabs.

    (A Lerner natural science book)
    Adaptation of: The lives of crabs/by Yasuyuki Koike.
    Includes index.
    Summary: Discusses the physical characteristics,
  behavior, and life cycle of crabs.
    1. Crabs—Juvenile literature. [1. Crabs] I. Sakurai,
  Atsushi, ill. II. Koike, Yasuyuki. Kani no kurashi.
  III. Title. IV. Series.

  QL444.M33J64   1982   595.3′842   82-10056
  ISBN 0-8225-1471-0 (lib. bdg.)

1 2 3 4 5 6 7 8 9 10   90 89 88 87 86 85 84 83 82

If you take a walk along a sandy ocean beach or a rocky shore, you will probably see some of the scurrying, long-legged creatures known as crabs. Crabs are **crustaceans,** animals whose soft bodies are protected by hard outer coverings. Other crustaceans like lobsters and shrimps make their homes in the ocean. Many kinds of crabs are ocean dwellers too, but some crabs live on land, while others divide their time between the water and the land.

This book describes those crabs that live in the special environment where land and water meet. It also takes a look at a few of the colorful crabs found in the world's oceans.

Many shore crabs are active during the dark hours of the night. They move rapidly over rocks and sand, searching for food.

THE PARTS OF A CRAB'S BODY

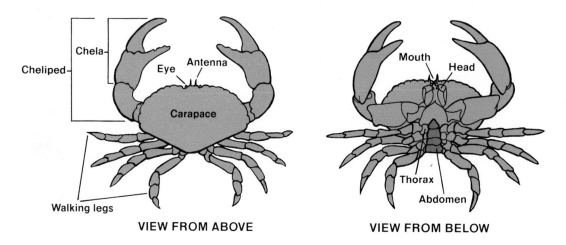

VIEW FROM ABOVE

VIEW FROM BELOW

Whether they spend most of their time on land or in the water, all crabs are alike in many ways. Their bodies have the same basic parts, and their lives follow the same general pattern of development and change.

There are three main parts to a crab's body, but these parts are not easy to see when you are looking at a crab in its normal upright position. The body parts are hidden under the large shell, or **carapace,** that the crab carries on its back. If you look at a crab that has been turned over on its back, you can see the three sections of its body more easily.

The head and the middle section, called the **thorax,** are joined together in a unit known as the **cephalothorax.** (**Cephalo** is a Greek word meaning "head.") In most crabs, the abdomen—the third section of the body—is folded back and tucked under the cephalothorax. It looks like a kind of curled-under tail.

Left: A crab's mouth is surrounded by parts used for tearing and crushing food. *Right:* The eyes of many crabs are located on the ends of stalks that can move in all directions.

All three parts of a crab's body are made up of small individual units or segments. You can see these segments in the drawing of a crab shown on the opposite page. In most crabs, each segment has a pair of jointed **appendages** attached to it. These appendages come in different sizes, and they serve several different purposes. Some of the small appendages on a crab's head work as mouthparts. They tear up pieces of food and put them into the crab's mouth.

Attached to the segments of a crab's thorax are five pairs of large appendages. These 10 strong, jointed limbs are the animal's legs. Lobsters and shrimps also have 10 legs. Because of this characteristic, all three kinds of crustaceans are often referred to as **decapods,** a word that means "10-footed."

Above: This swimming crab has paddles on its last pair of legs. Two of the crab's other legs are missing, but they will eventually be replaced by a remarkable process called regeneration. *Opposite:* Shore and land crabs can use their versatile legs to climb up reeds or even tall trees.

A crab uses most of its legs for transportation, just as other animals do. On the four back pairs of legs, crabs walk or run over the shore or along the ocean floor. Some crabs that live in the water have paddles on their last pair of legs that make them useful for swimming.

When a crab walks or runs, it usually moves sideways rather than straight forward. The four walking legs on one side of its body bend and pull the crab along, while the legs on the other side stretch out and push. Moving in this way, a crab can travel easily over rocks, sand, or even mud.

A CRAB'S CHELA

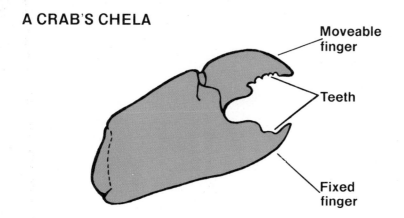

Moveable finger

Teeth

Fixed finger

A crab's first two legs, the ones closest to its head, are very special appendages. Although they are sometimes used for walking, their main purpose is to grasp and hold things. These two legs, which are often larger than the other eight, are called **chelipeds**. Each is equipped with a powerful claw or pincer known as a **chela**. A chela has two parts or fingers; one finger is moveable, while the other stays in a fixed position. Both fingers may have jagged teeth designed for cutting or for gripping objects firmly.

The object most often gripped in a crab's two chelae is something to eat. Crabs use their versatile claws to obtain many kinds of food. Crabs that live in the ocean capture small fish and shellfish. Other crabs use their chelae to scrape algae off of rocks. Crabs also feed on seaweed or green plants that grow near the shore. Some shore crabs are scavengers, collecting and eating dead fish and decaying plant material.

This shore crab is holding a dead fish in its claws.

A pebble crab

The crabs shown on these two pages have powerful chelae especially designed to open the shells of clams, snails, and other marine mollusks. The little pebble crab (above) uses its chelae to crack the shells of marine snails and to pull out the soft bodies hidden inside. The chelae then hold the snails up to the crab's mouth so that the mouthparts can go to work, tearing and shredding the food.

The box crab (opposite) has enormous chelae decorated with knobs and fringes of hair. This crab specializes in

14

chipping open mollusk shells. A box crab will grasp a marine snail in its walking legs while it uses the teeth on its chelae to chip small pieces out of the snail shell. Eventually the crab will make an opening large enough to pull the snail out of its protective covering.

A box crab can also use its chelae for protection. The large claws are designed to fold tightly against the front of the crab's body. When a box crab has its chelae in this position, as in the picture shown here, the soft parts of its body are completely surrounded by a "box" of hard shell. Box crabs have also earned the nickname bashful crabs because they seem to hide behind their huge claws.

A box crab

Opposite: A group of crabs feeding on a beach. *Right:* This ghost crab is surrounded by pellets of waste material left over after its meal.

Several groups of shore-dwelling crabs use their chelae in a very unusual way to obtain food. Among them are ghost crabs (pictured above) and fiddler crabs (shown on page 25). These crustaceans are known as **deposit feeders** because they feed on food material deposited in beach sand or mud.

The crabs use their spoon-shaped chelae to scoop up sand and put it into their mouths. The mouthparts sift through the sand, separating out tiny pieces of plant and animal material. Such food material is eaten, while the sand is formed into little balls and pushed out of the mouth.

As it eats, a deposit-feeding crab moves slowly along the beach, using its two claws one after the other to carry sand to its mouth. The crab leaves behind it a line of pellets containing the leftovers from its feast.

Crabs feeding on a beach make a tempting meal for shore birds like sandpipers (above) and longbills (opposite). Birds are only one of the kinds of animals that prey on crabs. In the sea, crabs may be hunted and eaten by predators such as fish and octopuses. Sometimes crabs even attack and eat each other.

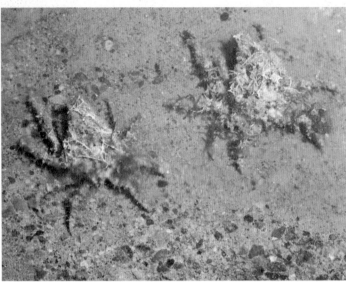

Left: **A hairy crab.** *Right:* **Crabs camouflaged with seaweed.**

Crabs have many ways of protecting themselves from attacks by the animals that prey on them. One of the best ways is the use of camouflage.

Many crabs are naturally camouflaged because their colors or textures blend in well with the environment in which they live. The bodies of ghost crabs are often a pale color that is almost invisible against the background of a sandy beach. Hairy crabs have hairs on their carapaces and legs that pick up bits of mud and plants. Wearing these shaggy coats, the crabs blend in with the plant growth on the beach or ocean floor.

Other kinds of crabs make disguises out of the material around them. Some chop up seaweed with their claws and pile it on their carapaces. Others called decorator crabs neatly arrange pieces of broken shells on their carapaces.

The sponge crab (above) cuts off a piece of sponge to just
the right size and puts it on the carapace, holding the sponge
in place with its two back legs.

This ghost crab has very long eye stalks that give it a wide range of vision. The stalks can be lowered into sockets on the carapace to protect the crab's eyes.

Hiding is also a good way to avoid predators. In the picture above, a ghost crab is hidden under the shallow water along the shore. Only its eye stalks are uncovered, sticking up like two periscopes. The picture on the right shows a ghost crab feeding in the sand.

Left: **This shore crab is digging a hole in the sand with its back legs.** *Right:* **With most of its body buried in the sand, the crab keeps an eye on its surroundings.**

Many crabs hide themselves in burrows and holes. When they are frightened, some shore crabs will quickly dig a hole in the sand with their legs and bury themselves in it. Other crabs have permanent burrows that serve as their homes.

Fiddler crabs like the one shown on the opposite page often have deep burrows dug into the beach sand. These shelters are located in the area between the lines of high and low tide. When the tide is at its low mark, fiddlers come out of their burrows and search for food on the wet sand. If an enemy approaches, a crab will hurry back to its burrow and hide until the danger passes.

When the ocean tide begins to rise, a fiddler crab goes into its burrow and plugs the entrance with pellets of sand. The rising water covers the burrow, but the crab is sealed inside, safe in the chamber at the bottom.

Above: A fiddler crab near the entrance of its burrow. *Below:* A cross-section of the fiddler's burrow.

This coral crab is holding two anemones in its claws.

If a crab cannot hide or disguise itself to avoid a predator, then it may have to defend itself in a more direct manner. Many crabs will wave their claws in the air if they are threatened. This display of strength may serve to frighten a predator away. If not, the claws can be used as weapons to pinch and nip an enemy.

Some crabs use borrowed weapons to threaten predators. The most popular weapons of ocean-dwelling crabs are **sea anemones,** soft-bodied creatures that have a stinging poison in their tentacles. One tiny crab that lives in the coral reefs of the Pacific Ocean actually picks up anemones in its claws and waves them at potential attackers.

Other crabs collect sea anemones from the ocean floor and put them on their carapaces. The anemones attach themselves to the shells and ride around with the crabs as they go about their business. The passengers do not harm their hosts, but predators usually stay away from crabs carrying stinging anemones on their backs. The anemones benefit because they get to eat some of the crabs' leftover food.

● A crab waving its claws to frighten an enemy

Threatened by a human attacker, this crab has broken off one of its claws.

Despite all their means of protection, crabs are often caught by predators. When this happens, a crab has one last defense. If a predator has grabbed an appendage, the crab can break off that appendage and scurry away. The crab escapes, and the attacker is left holding the broken-off limb.

This escape act is possible because a crab's appendages have built-in **breaking planes,** points at which breakage can occur without injuring the crab. When a crab is seized by one of its legs, it tightens its muscles in such a way that the leg breaks off at the breaking plane. The stump of the leg has a kind of seal that prevents blood and other body fluids from escaping.

Crabs use this break-away method not only to escape predators but also to get rid of damaged appendages. The system is a practical one because once an appendage has been shed, it is automatically replaced by a new one.

The bud of a new leg (right) begins to form soon after the old leg has been broken off. It grows larger gradually (below) until it is the same size as the lost limb. This amazing process of replacement is called **regeneration.**

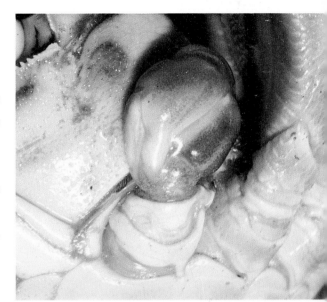

At mating time, land crabs move toward the shore. They must be near the water during this important period of their lives.

A pair of crabs mating. The male is the larger of the two.

Crabs can replace lost limbs by means of regeneration. A more complicated process is needed to produce a whole new crab.

Like most animals, crabs create more of their own kind through the process of sexual reproduction. The sex cells of male and female crabs must be united in order for new life to begin. To get ready for this union, many shore crabs go through special courtship ceremonies. Male crabs wave their claws to attract females of their species. Some males make drumming sounds by tapping their claws on rocks.

When a male finds a willing female of his species, the two crabs mate. In the act of mating, male sex cells, or sperm, pass from the male's body into the female's body. When the sperm unite with, or fertilize, the female's eggs, new life begins to develop.

31

Above: A female crab carrying a mass of eggs on the underside of her body. *Opposite:* Female crabs entering the water to release their eggs.

Not long after mating, most female shore crabs are ready to lay their eggs. A female crab produces thousands of tiny eggs, each one much smaller than the period at the end of this sentence. The eggs leave the female's body through openings near the end of the thorax. Covered with a jelly-like substance, the eggs cling together in a mass that sticks to the underside of the female's body, between her thorax and abdomen. The folded-up abdomen is pushed away from the body to form a kind of cradle for the egg mass.

Depending on the species, a female crab carries her eggs around with her from two weeks to several months. During this time, shore and land crabs stay near the water, for the eggs must be kept moist during their development. When the time comes for the eggs to hatch, the females enter the shallow water near the shore.

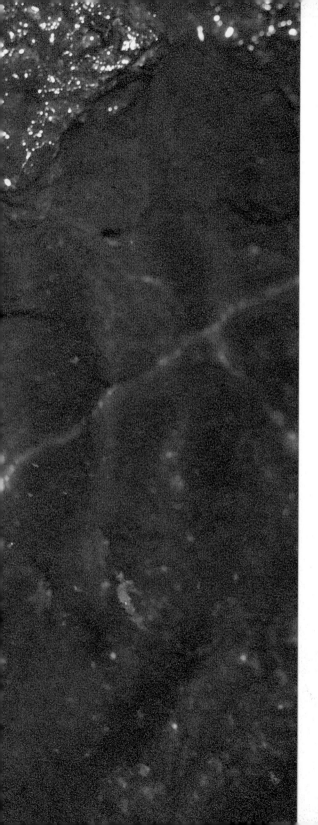

In the water, the female crab moves her abdomen rapidly from side to side. This movement helps to break open the thousands of egg cases. The creatures that emerge from the eggs are crab **larvae,** and they don't resemble adult crabs at all. Like a frog tadpole or a butterfly caterpillar, a crab larva must go through a series of changes before it finally becomes an adult.

35

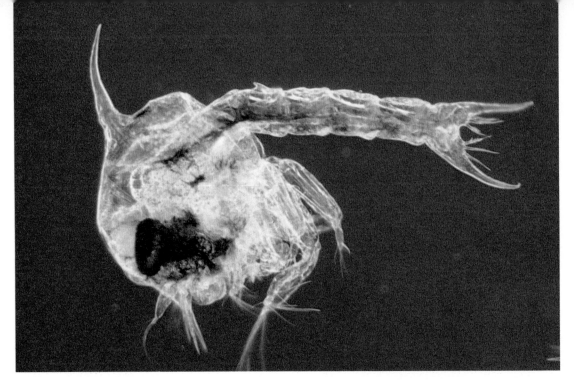

After it hatches, a crab larva is called a zoea. The zoea in this picture is about 1 millimeter (1/25 inch) long.

All crab larvae are creatures of the sea, even though they may have hatched from eggs laid by land-dwelling crabs. The larvae go through the different stages of their development in the water, breathing with gills and swimming with the help of their fringed legs.

There are two main stages in the development of a crab larva. During the first stage, the larva is known as a **zoea.** A zoea is very tiny and looks more like a shrimp than an adult crab. This little creature feeds mainly on the larvae of other sea animals like oysters and starfish. It grows rapidly by means of **molting,** or shedding the hard outer covering of its body and growing a new covering. A zoea usually

A megalops is the second stage in a crab's larval development. This megalops is about 10 millimeters (1/4 inch) long.

molts four times, and at each molt, more appendages are added to its body.

By the time the larva enters the second stage of its development, it has begun to look a lot more like its parents. Now it is known as a **megalops,** a word that means "large eyes." A megalops does have enormous eyes, and it also has the claws and the other appendages of an adult crab. Its larval development is almost finished.

After it becomes a megalops, a crab larva molts one more time. The larvae of ocean-dwelling crabs go through this final molt on the ocean floor. Land and shore crabs usually come out of the water at this important time of their lives.

Above: A megalops molting. *Opposite:* A young crab is smaller than an adult and usually a lighter color.

When the megalops molts, it emerges as a young crab, with all the basic body parts of an adult. Its larval development is complete, but the new little crab will continue to grow in size. In order to grow, a crab must continue to molt throughout its life.

The covering of a crab's body, including its carapace, is made of a hard material called **chitin.** This covering protects the crab's soft body parts and also acts as an external skeleton, providing a framework for the body. A crab's **exoskeleton** is a very useful device, but it has one drawback: it cannot change in size. The exoskeleton must be discarded in order for a crab to grow larger. This is what happens when a crab molts.

When a crab is ready to molt, a split develops in the area where the carapace joins the abdomen (above). The crab slowly backs out through this opening, leaving its old exoskeleton behind (right). Underneath, a new body covering has already formed, but at this point, it is still soft and stretches easily.

After it has molted, a crab takes large amounts of water into its body. The water stretches out the soft new exoskeleton to its full size before it hardens. As the crab begins to eat and grow, the water is replaced by expanding body tissue. The crab will continue growing until it reaches the size limit of its new exoskeleton. Then it will be time to molt again.

Because they grow rapidly, young crabs molt often, perhaps once every 10 days. Adult crabs usually molt only once or twice a year. The time of molting is a very dangerous period in a crab's life. While its new exoskeleton is still soft, a crab's body is unprotected from attacks by predators. Most crabs hide themselves from sight until their new body coverings have hardened.

The hermit crab sheds its exoskeleton regularly, just like other crabs. But this crustacean has a different kind of protective covering that must also be replaced.

Hermit crabs have special molting requirements because of their unusual body construction, which sets them apart from "true" crabs like ghosts and fiddlers. Instead of having a small abdomen that is folded under the thorax, a hermit crab has a large abdomen that extends out at the end of its body. The most unusual thing about a hermit crab's abdomen is that it does not have a hard outer covering. A hermit's cephalothorax and appendages are covered by an exoskeleton, but its abdomen lacks this important protection.

Hermit crabs make up for this lack by sticking their soft abdomens inside hard shells that originally belonged to other sea creatures. As soon as a young hermit develops to the adult stage, it must look for a shell house of the proper size. A hermit crab's abdomen has a curved shape that fits perfectly inside the spiral shells of marine snails like whelks and conchs. The crab carries its borrowed shell around by holding it from the inside with its two back legs. Its claws and walking legs stick out the shell's opening.

A hermit crab with its bright red legs sticking out the opening of its borrowed shell

Like other crabs, the hermit crab must shed its exoskeleton in order to grow larger. It must also replace its shell house periodically to accommodate its growing body. At molting time, a hermit crab looks for a larger shell. The crab pulls its abdomen out of the old shell and backs into its new, roomier accommodations.

Some hermit crabs live on shore and find housing in shells that have been washed up by the waves and tides. Hermits that live in the sea often gather in large groups on the ocean floor in areas where snail shells are abundant. Many other kinds of crabs are also at home in the ocean ...

River crabs like the ones shown in this picture live in freshwater rivers and streams rather than in the salty waters of the ocean.

Most of the crabs that people use for food live in the waters of the sea. Blue crabs are found in the Atlantic, off the coast of North America. The large king crab comes from the cold waters of the North Pacific. Both of these kinds of crabs are caught in large numbers by commercial fishing companies. The meat taken from the crabs' claws and legs is eaten and enjoyed by people all over the world.

Some of the most interesting of the ocean-dwelling crabs are colorful coral crabs like the ones shown on the opposite page. These little crustaceans live among the coral reefs found in the warm waters of tropical oceans. Many coral crabs get their food from **coral polyps,** the tiny animals that create the hard limestone material of a coral reef. The crabs use their feet and claws to scratch and poke the coral polyps inside their limestone houses. Irritated in this way, the polyps produce a sticky mucus that the crabs scrape up and eat. By their peculiar feeding habits, coral crabs may help the polyps to get rid of dirt and debris.

Coral crabs are as brightly colored as the tropical fish and other sea creatures that make their homes in a coral reef.

GLOSSARY

appendages (uh-PEN-dij-uhs)—small body parts connected to the main section of an animal's body. Most crabs have 19 pairs of appendages, including their mouthparts and legs.

breaking planes—points on a crab's appendages where breakage can occur without injuring the crab

carapace (KARE-uh-pase)—the large shell covering the top of a crab's body

cephalothorax (sef-uh-luh-THOR-aks)—a body unit made up of the joined head and thorax

chela (KEE-luh)—a claw on one of a crab's front legs, used for grasping and holding objects. The plural form of the word is **chelae**, pronounced KEE-lee.

chelipeds (KEE-luh-peds)—legs that end in claws or chelae

chitin (KITE-uhn)—a hard material that makes up most of a crab's carapace and the other coverings of its body

coral polyps (PAHL-ips)—soft-bodied animals that produce the limestone material of a coral reef. Coral polyps are related to jellyfish, sea anemones, and other marine creatures with soft bodies.

crustaceans (krus-TAY-shuns)—animals like crabs, lobsters, and shrimps that have segmented bodies covered with a hard protective material. Crustaceans belong to the scientific class Crustacea.

decapods (DEK-uh-pods)—crustaceans that have 10 legs. Decapods are members of the order Decapoda.

deposit feeders—crabs that get their food from material deposited in sand or mud

exoskeleton (ek-so-SKEL-ih-tun)—the hard outer covering of a crustacean's body, which provides protection and support to the soft body parts

larvae (LAR-vee)—immature crabs after hatching and before developing into adults. The singular form of the word is **larva,** pronounced LAR-vuh.

megalops (MEG-uh-lops)—a crab larva in the second stage of its development

molting—shedding the outer covering of the body to make way for a new covering

regeneration (ree-jen-ih-RAY-shun)—the growth of a new body part to replace one that has been lost

sea anemones (uh-NEM-uh-nees)—animals with soft, cylinder-shaped bodies topped by stinging tentacles. Sea anemones often have a flower-like appearance and are named after the bright-colored flowers called anemones.

thorax (THOR-aks)—the middle section of a crab's body

zoea (zo-EE-uh)—a crab larva in the first stage of its development

INDEX